Bermuda:
Everything You Need To Know When Traveling to Bermuda.

Table Of Contents

Copyright

Introduction

I want to thank you and congratulate you for downloading the book, *"Bermuda: Everything You Need To Know When Traveling to Bermuda."*

This book contains everything you need to know to plan the perfect trip to Bermuda.

(In this Bermuda travel guide you will learn everything you need to know before you set out on your Bermuda travels. From the history of Bermuda to the myths and facts surrounding the triangle nothing will be left uncovered. You will also learn about all the activities and sights you can see when traveling in Bermuda as well as tips and warnings for you trip. Let this be your Bermuda guide book as you enjoy your travels.)

Thanks again for downloading this book, I hope you enjoy it!

History of Bermuda
The Discovery of Bermuda

Discovered in 1505 by Juan de Bermudez the island was called La Bermuda. In 1515 Bermudez attempted a second visit to La Bermuda but due to the weather conditions was unable to land.

In 1609 the Sea Venture was leading a fleet of nine to Jamestown Virginia which was bringing much needed provisions to the settlers. The entire fleet was caught in a storm and the Sea Venture was driven off course. It had to be driven up onto the East Bermuda reefs in order to save it from sinking and to save the lives of the passengers.

There were 150 sailors and settlers on board the Sea Venture as well as one dog. They stayed for 10 months in Bermuda. When the Sea Venture's longboard was rigged with a mast and sent in search of Jamestown, many of the survivors were lost at sea and the ship was never seen again.

Those of the survivors that were left decided to build two new ships. The first ship that was built was called the Deliverance and was built out of what could be salvaged from the Sea Venture which was still sitting on the reef. The second ship called the Patience was made completely out of material found on the island. The Deliverance was made so that those who were still stuck in Bermuda could travel to Jamestown but the Patience had to be built in order to carry supplies and food that the survivors had stockpiled to get them through the trip.

When the survivors finished building both of the ships most of them sat sail to Jamestown finally finishing their voyage. When the survivors reached Jamestown they found that most of the colonies population had been annihilated by "The Starving Time".

There were only 60 survivors left out of the original 500 settlers and most of them were dying from disease. The supplies that the Deliverance brought with it was far too little to help the colony survive and those who were left decided it was best to return to England but were prevented from returning due to the arrival of another relief fleet.

Those that were left of the Sea Venture survivors had brought back pork with them from pigs they had killed while in Bermuda which led the Jamestown colonists to refer to currency as Bermuda hogs. Some of these survivors returned to Bermuda in order to gather more supplies for the colonies but ended up dying due to the pork.

Two volunteers were left in Bermuda when the Deliverance left for Jamestown the first time and one more was left when the Patience returned in order to maintain England claim to the island. Since that time the island has always been in habited and dates its origin back to 1609 and not 1612 when it was declared an official settlement.

In 1612 sixty settlers were sent to Bermuda to join the three volunteers already there. The 63 settlers founded and began construction on what is now known as the town of St. George.

In 1620 a representative government was introduced in Bermuda and Bermuda's House of Assembly held their first meeting which allowed Bermuda to become a self-governing colony.

The early colony of Bermuda
In the beginning the only crop that was grown in Bermuda was tobacco although investors repeatedly advised against it. Investors wanted to see more crops grown in Bermuda because there were so many risks involved when living in a single crop economy and because the quality of the tobacco grown in Bermuda was very low. Often investors or "The Company" found themselves burning the tobacco shipments that came to England from Bermuda because of the low quality.

It took a while for the settlers of Bermuda to move away from growing tobacco as their only crop and to stop using it as a form of currency. Many of the islanders turned to shipbuilding as well as maritime trade but The Company could not make any money unless the land was under cultivation so it was forbidden for any vessel to be made without having the proper license. This interference in the livelihood of the Bermuda settlers eventually caused the dissolution of The Company in 1684.

Slavery

Even though the first slaves were brought to Bermuda early in the establishment of the colony, the agricultural economy did not become dependent upon it.

Unlike the plantation economy that was developing the North America, Bermuda used an indentured servant system which provided an abundance of cheap labor. This resulted in the Saxon to remain the majority despite the constant influx of Latino's, Black's, Native American's, Irish, and Scots.

The first Blacks to immigrate to Bermuda were West Indians, they were free and were leaving territories that had been taken from Spain. Upon arrival to Bermuda they worked for seven years as indentured servants as most settlers did at the time to pay The Company back for the cost of transportation. The black population in Bermuda began to grow and many attempt were made by The Company to reduce it and one of these attempts was to raise the years of indentured servitude to 99 years for blacks.

There were also many slaves that were brought to Bermuda by privateers and these slaves could be obtained by purchasing them privately or at auctions, they could be taken if the owner owed a debt and were used as payment for the debt, and they could also be given as gifts.
During that time period you could buy a young black child for what would equal to about 13 dollars today. A woman was sold for what would equal anywhere between 16 and 32 dollars today and able bodied black man was sold for what would equal 42 dollars today.

The blacks and Indians that were kept as slaves in Bermuda never accepted their status as slaves and took every opportunity they could find to try and escape even though this was not an easy task due to the size of the island and the fact that the closest land mass is over 700 miles away. Nevertheless, the slaves would escape and live in caves on the island.

During this time many slaves also tried to rebel against their masters and many tried to seek revenge against them. One plot of revenge took place in 1656 when over a dozen black men plotted to kill their English masters. It is said that just hours before the murders were to take place two of the slaves involved lost their nerve and reported the plot to authorities. Everyone involved was gathered up and tried by the court martial.

The two slaves who reported the plot were set free while five of the involved slaves were branded, had their noses slit and were beaten before they were executed. The rest of the slaves involved were beaten and branded before being released back to their masters.

The result of this plot of slaves wanting to kill their masters caused slave owners to want stricter laws concerning their slaves. In 1674 laws were passed which stated that any slave that was found off of their master's property without the proper ticket could be beaten or whipped. If the slaves were to be found a second time they would have one of their ears cut of and if a third offence happened they would be beaten until their skin was broken and branded.

Many Native Americans were also brought to Bermuda as slaves during this time and it is reported that they were preferred over blacks and Irish as house servants because they caused less problems and did not try to raise up a rebellion as the black slaves did.

Between 1641 and 1659 England forced over 350,000 Irish men, women and children to become slaves in Bermuda but upon learning that the Irish were plotting against their masters with the black slaves, the import of Irish slaves was banned.

In 1807 slave trade was outlawed in Bermuda and all of the slaves were set free 1834. At this time blacks and Native Americans were the minority in Bermuda but just before the United States gained its independence, many of the white English settlers of Bermuda immigrated to the US which left the blacks as the majority. Today over 60% of the population claim to be descendants of Africa and most of the population can trace their heritage back to Africa and Europe.

After slavery was outlawed, many worked in maritime, ship building and those who were the most unfortunate worked in salt raking in Turks Island.

The Turks Island, Salt and Bermuda.

The Turk Islands also called the Salt islands were not colonized until 1681 when salt collectors from Bermuda first settled there. The salt collectors were attracted to Turk Island because of the shallow waters it offered allowing salt collection to be much easier than it was in Bermuda. The settlers only stayed on the Turk Island six months out of each year and returned to Bermuda during the off season when they were unable to rake salt.

In order to develop the salt industry, the Bermudians completely destroyed the natural habitat of Turk Island. They cut down all of the trees in order to stop rain fall which would interfere with salt collecting and to this day this damage has not been fully repaired. Bermuda suffered the same deforestation due to its ship building industry

Much of the 18th century was spent fighting legal battles over the Turk Island with the Bahamas. During this time no colony was allowed to own a colony of its own and although the Bahamas were colonized by Bermudians, Bermuda and the Bahamas fought over who had the rights to the Turk Island. According to England the Turk Island was not a colony and was seen like a river is seen today, for the common use of all which caused a lot of turmoil surrounding the ownership of the Turk Island.

In 1776 Turk Island was allowed to govern itself but continued to struggle with the Bahamas which continually tried to tax any salt raker on the Turk Island and even went as far as arresting those who were found raking for salt on the island. Eventually the English government handed over control of the island to the Bahamians but by that time all of the Bermudians had left. Because of the problems that the Bahamians had caused when seizing ships full of salt, and a hurricane that destroyed most of the salt reserves, the US had found other sources to buy their salt from and there was no longer a demand for the Bermudians to rake the island any longer.

American Independence and Bermuda.
American winning its independence from England led to great changes for Bermuda. Before the war, Bermuda was left to its own devices by the English government which allowed the shaping of the colonies by those who settled in Bermuda.

During this time the English government still had a Governor in Bermuda but the real power on the island was held by the wealthiest families who dominated the economy and who had the most political power because they filled the benches of the House of Assembly and the Privy Council.

Bermuda merchants sat up ports in what would become the Southern States of the US in order to achieve a leading position in merchant trading.

When Bermuda lost Turk Island, they had to diversify their trades widely in order to succeed. The Bermudians took up logging, merchant shipping, fishing, whaling and privateering. And as Bermuda focused more and more on the sea, they became more dependent on the food shipments from the US colonies and became their main trading partner.

When the 13 colonies rebelled, those in Bermuda sympathized with them because of the strong bonds that had been built between the two. When trade with the colonies was banned by England, those in Bermuda were facing the possibility of starvation because they traded their salt which the colonies depended on for food from the colonies. Although it was illegal the Bermudians continued to trade with the colonies and it is said that had they not been so far away they would have been the 14th colony to join the rebellion.

After the war was over England began to focus much more on the island because it was the only land they had that would protect their trade routes and allowed the royal navy to operate in the area. Due to the navy setting up bases in Bermuda there was no longer a need for privateers on the island and it quickly died out. And since America had become a foreign land Bermuda trade merchants were seriously harmed. America had also found new salt suppliers which caused the salt trade in Bermuda to fall upon hard times.

Bermuda's maritime trades as well as their ship building industry slowly died due to ships no longer being built from wood.

By the end of the 19th century those living in Bermuda and around the world viewed Bermuda as completely opposite of what it was before the American War of Independence.

Tourism in Bermuda

It was during the Victorian period when tourism first developed in Bermuda. Those who toured Bermuda at this time were the wealthiest of the United States who came to Bermuda in order to escape the cold winter months of North America. Many of the tourists also came in search of young aristocrats who worked at the naval bases that would be interested in marrying their daughters.

The locals were very quick to exploit this holding festivals and dances during the "tourist season" and giving invitations to the naval officers. Due to the fact that many men had moved from Bermuda because of the failure of the maritime industry history shows that there was a high population of women in Bermuda at the time. These women usually married the men who worked on the naval base but due to women coming from America they found that they had to compete with them.

By the 20th century Bermuda was attracting even more tourism. Much of the wealthy in the US, Canada, and England were visiting Bermuda on a regular basis. This helped the economy of Bermuda since they no longer were allowed to export to the US they spent much of their time focusing on growing the business of tourism.

Bermuda's economy flourished after the Second World War and although it still greatly depends on tourism it has been successful at building an offshore financial center.

Chapter 2
Bermuda Triangle Myths and Facts

There are so many myths that focus around the Bermuda Triangle and for that reason many are attracted to Bermuda. It is also one reason many people avoid the area all together. In this chapter we are going to learn some of the amazing stories that surround the Bermuda Triangle and then we will learn the facts about the area.

The record of strange occurrences surrounding the Bermuda Triangle go all the way back to the time of Columbus. There are reports that his compass would read wrong when traveling near the area. Many times this has been depicted in movies as the compass spinning in circles but the fact is that it merely points the wrong direction.

There have been many unexplained disappearances in the Bermuda Triangle and even though many reporters and scientists have tried to explain them some of the disappearances still seem unexplainable.

One of the most well-known stories is about Flight 19 which disappeared during US Navy training exercises. It was December of 1945 and on a routine mission five bombers left Fort Lauderdale but after several radio messages were sent, 14 crew members disappeared. A search plane was sent out to find the bombers only to disappear itself. It is not known what exactly went wrong with the mission but it is recorded that the weather was bad and the compass was showing the wrong direction so the pilots decided to navigate by landmarks. There was an unexpected storm which broke off radio communications and even though searches have been attempted no wreckage has ever been found.

Another amazing story involves the ship the Mary Celeste. The ship was found on December 4, 1872 and none of the crew members were on board. Upon investigation it was found that everything on the ship was still intact and there were no items missing. Even the barrels of alcohol were still on board ruling out pirates. Many speculated about why an entire crew would abandon their ship and some of the ideas included that the crew went crazy and jumped overboard, sea quakes and pirate attacks. None of the ideas about why the ship was abandoned made any sense, no one could understand why an entire crew would abandon an undamaged ship on a sunny day. To this day there are no answers as to what happened to the crew and no remains were ever found.

The Ellen Austin was a ship that was bound for New York in 1881. The ship was stumbled upon a deserted ship and found that the ship was in perfect condition minus the crew. In order to tow the deserted ship back a prize crew was placed on the ship and the two ships sat sail. A sharp increase in wind speed separated the two ships and those aboard the Ellen Austin reported that the ship suddenly disappeared. The Ellen Austin immediately sailed back to London. It was reported that the deserted ship was seen once again but had a different crew on it than what the Ellen Austin reported putting on the ship. The disappearance, reappearance and missing crews all make for an intriguing story but is it a story or is it the mystery of the Bermuda Triangle?

Another such story involving a ship involves the USS Cyclops. The ship carried 309 crew members and set sail in March of 1918. The day was clear and only one message was every received from the ship. They did not indicated problems or distress from the crew members and it was never heard from again. A search was put together to find the 309 crew members but not one was ever found nor was any wreckage of the ship. This still remains a mystery today because like the Mary Celeste, no reason seems to fit as to why the ship would just disappear.

In 1921 an investigation team was sent to Barbados in order to search for Carroll A. Deering who was wanted for rum running. However what the team found was a ship whose crew was missing. It is reported that nine vessels disappeared during this time period or their crews went missing. Although finding the few ships that have been found give some insight into the happenings at the Bermuda triangle, they give no definite answers and have not brought anyone any closer to solving any of these mysteries.

In December of 1967 a cabin cruiser set off with its captain. The name of the cruiser was the Witchcraft. Within a few minutes after setting off the coastguard received a call for help from the captain Dan Burrack who stated that he had hit something large but there was no damage to the boat. Not wanting to take any risks the coast guard sent out a rescue team and arrived within 19 minutes of the call coming in. What was found only created more questions. There was no boat anywhere in sight. What puzzled the rescue team was that this type of boat was virtually unsinkable, no life raft was found and no life vest was used. The boat just disappeared and to this day no evidence of the boat was ever found.

On average 4 aircrafts and 20 yachts go missing in the Bermuda Tringle each year. There are many theories as to why there are so many disappearances in the Bermuda Triangle and I would love to discuss a few of them with you.

One of the theories is that the Bermuda Triangle is where Atlantis used to be. Many speculate that the people of Atlantis used crystals as a way to create huge amounts of energy and they believe that it is these crystals that are causing so many disappearances in the Bermuda Triangle. Those who believe in this theory suggest that the power of the crystals is actually destroying the ships as they pass overhead. No such crystals have ever been found in the area and everyone knows that no location for Atlantis has ever been found so this theory is unsubstantiated.

Another theory that people believe explains the disturbing events surrounding the Bermuda Triangle is UFO's. Of course blaming alien beings is irresistible to many people when something happens that cannot be explained by science. In Steven Spielberg's Close Encounters of the Third Kind, the crew of Flight 19 are found with aliens and kindly returned to earth. But many people actually do believe that for some reason alien beings are abducting those who travel through the Bermuda Triangle in order to run tests on them and use them for experiments. Although this is a fascinating theory it of course has never been proven as extraterrestrial life has never been found on any planet.

There are also theories that discuss a comet crashing in the Bermuda Triangle over 11,000 years ago. It is thought that this comet could somehow affect the electromagnetic field in the area and cause the disappearances. In 1979 John Hutchinson conducted experiments with electromagnetic fields and was able to make metal float on water, make water swirl in a cup, melt metal, and break glass among many other strange events. Hutchinson theorized that if he was able to create such events in a controlled environment than nature would have no problem creating the same type of events whenever and wherever it pleased. He believed that this was the explanation for the strange fog that is reportedly seen in the Bermuda Triangle as well.

There are also those who believe that it is a conspiracy by the government who has an underwater naval base in the area. They believe this is why there have been no real scientific tests of the area. This cannot be proven correct or incorrect because of the fact that there are no proper experiments being conducted at the site. It is also believed that disappearances in the Bermuda Triangle are no longer publicized because the government does not want the people to become interested in the area once again.

Some also believe that the Bermuda Triangle is a type of portal that leads to a parallel universe. They believe that the Bermuda Triangle is like a door way that leads from this diminution to the next. They believe that those who travel through the door have no idea what is going on at the time and that when they travel to the parallel universe they no longer age.

Of course most of these theories sound like nothing more than fairy tales and cannot be proven true so what really is happening in the Bermuda Triangle. Now it is time to look at the facts.

The truth is that there are high levels of methane gas in the ocean where the Bermuda Triangle is located. This could actually account for why the ships disappear but not the planes or people. You see when methane gas rises to the surface of the ocean, the surface becomes unstable. Anything that is sitting on the surface suddenly weighs more than the water in the ocean therefore it quickly sinks to the bottom. Studies have proven that this is also possible with simple oxygen bubbles but the sinking happens a lot slower than it does with methane gas bubbles. If this is what is causing the ships to disappear how can the missing crews and airplanes be explained?

The swift current of the Gulf Stream which runs through the Bermuda Triangle can quickly rid the area of any debris that would be left from a crash. In fact, the Mary Celeste although said that the crew vanished in the Bermuda Triangle was actually found off of the coast of Africa. The stream is swift enough to move a ship across the entire ocean therefore it is definitely swift enough to rid the area of debris. The weather in the area is very unpredictable as well. Strong storms can suddenly appear as well as water spouts. This causes new hazards to form in the ocean very quickly. This also can confuse the crew of a ship very easily and the fact that the Bermuda Triangle is one of only two places in the world where a compass does not point true north can confuse them even more.

The truth is that when you compare the Bermuda Triangle to any other location in the ocean you will see that they have around the same number of such strange occurrences recorded. People just hear more about what has happened in the Bermuda Triangle because of the "mystery" surrounding the area. You should also know that each and every day cruises and airplanes pass through the area and none of them have mysteriously disappeared and none of the passengers have either.

It is unknown what caused the incidents in the Bermuda Triangle, whether you believe there is something out there that is paranormal causing these events or if you believe there is a scientific explanation is completely a personal decision but the fact remains that you should never feel insecure about traveling through the area if you have an experienced pilot or captain.

Chapter 3 Bermuda Attractions

There are so many wonderful sites to see when you visit Bermuda. Knowing the history of these sites is often what makes them so wonderful so in this chapter we are going to discuss the many beautiful attractions and even discuss some gems that the regular touring community does not know about.

The Beaches

With 34 beaches available to visit in Bermuda it can be hard to decide which ones you want to spend your time at. Some are small and secluded and some even offer beautiful pink sand so here is a rundown of the top beaches in Bermuda.

- Horseshoe Bay- This beach has been ranked one of the top in the world by several international magazines. Located on the south shore this is one of the beautiful pink sand beaches in Bermuda. Being the most popular beach in Bermuda it is very crowded but there is a trail that leads east and if you follow it you can find much more secluded areas of the beach.
- Warwick Long Bay- Also located on the south shore this beach is relatively secluded and has several trails that you can follow to other beaches. This beach is also known for the beautiful pink sand and is about a mile long.
- Elbow Beach- Although part of the beach is owned by the Elbow Beach hotel the public part of the beach is just as amazing. The beach offers reefs nearby that can be enjoyed while snorkeling, and even a ship wreck that you can explore!
- Tobacco Bay- Even though this beach does not offer the pink sand as many of the other beaches in Bermuda do, it is still an amazing beach. The many rock formations make a great environment for fish and along with the very colorful marine life there are also many corals which makes for a great snorkeling experience.

- Hog Bay- This is one of the many hidden gems that you will find in this book. Hog Bay is a little known beach and is overlooked by most when visiting Bermuda. The beach is only accessible during low tide so it is very important that you time your visit to the beach well but once you get there you will most likely have the entire beach to yourself.
- John Smith's Bay- Offers a beautiful reef line just 200 yards off the shore this beach is also great for snorkeling. The reef keeps the water calm as well as keeps the boats a way making this a great beach for the family. There is also a life guard on duty during the summer months.

There are so many more beaches available that an entire book could be written about them alone but these are the best beaches you will find. Here is a list of the other beaches available for you to explore.

- ✓ Astwood Cove
- ✓ Jobson's Cove
- ✓ Church Bay
- ✓ Daniels Head
- ✓ Chaplin Bay
- ✓ Stonehole Bay
- ✓ Shelly Bay
- ✓ Whale Bay
- ✓ Snorkel Park
- ✓ Somerset Long Bay
- ✓ Achilles Bay
- ✓ St. Catherine
- ✓ Clearwater
- ✓ Devonshire
- ✓ Clarence Cove
- ✓ Deep Bay
- ✓ Bailey's Bay and Coney Island

Top Sites to Visit in Bermuda

Even though Bermuda is not that big and you can travel the entire length of the island in two hours by taxi there are tons of amazing sites to be seen. Here are the top sites for you to visit while you are traveling in Bermuda.

- Bermuda Aquarium, Museum & Zoo- Known to the locals as BAMZ this is one of the favorite attractions in Bermuda. Founded in 1926 BAMZ offers three attractions all in one complex. It usually takes around three hours to enjoy the entire attraction and there are even free one hour guided tours that you can take advantage of. The aquarium is the main attraction and the 140,000 gallon is the main focus and Contains the largest living coral collection in the world. There are over 100 species housed in the aquarium as well as an outdoor pool for harbor seals. You can spend some time watching the seal feedings and then enjoy a brief presentation afterwards. The museum has recently undergone renovations and now houses more displays than ever before. You can learn about Bermuda before humans ever arrived to the island as well as the impact that humans have had on the island and what is being done to preserve the island today. Although the Zoo is quite small they have done an amazing job setting up the habitats to be as close to how the animal would live in the wild as possible. There is even an area where you can interact with nature which features a touch pool, a glass encased beehive and many other features that allow you to interact.
- Crystal Caves- At about 120 feet below sea level this cave was discovered in 1905. Two young boys were trying to find their lost ball when the noticed it had dropped into a large hole and one of the boys went into the hole to retrieve the ball. As the boy traveled deeper into the hole he realized it was no hole at all but an amazing cave.

Today you don't have to crawl through a hole to enter the cave because a new entrance has been created. There are guided tours of the cave were you will learn about the history of the cave and all of the formations in the cave. It takes about thirty minutes for the entire tour of the cave and you will be able to enjoy the amazing walls that look like waterfalls frozen in time.

- The Bermuda Maritime Museum- Officially opened in 1975 and covering more than 30 acres this museum is dedicated to the history of maritime in Bermuda. Housed in the same building is the Dolphin Quest which offers interactive programs with the dolphins.
- St. Peter's Church- The church is located in Georgetown and it is believed that this is the oldest church that has been in continual use in the Western hemisphere. The current building however is not the first church that was built on the site and replaced the church that was built in 1612 because it was damaged during a storm. Inside the church you will be able to view many of the amazing treasures it has to offer including an alter from the original church that was built in 1615 and is the oldest piece of woodwork found in Bermuda. You will also be able to take in the simple elegance of the front of the church which was built over 500 years ago. In the church yard you will be able to view two graveyards. There was one area that was used for black slaves and another area was used to bury whites. There is also a separate gallery that was used by the blacks so that they could attend church. Behind the church you can also see a 500 year old tree that once held the church bell.

- Gibbs Hill Lighthouse- At 245 feet above sea level at the base of the light house and standing 177 feet high, Gibbs Hill Lighthouse is one of the main attractions in the Southampton parish. Built in 1848 this is the oldest cast iron lighthouse in the world. Climbing 185 steps will allow you to see Bermuda in an amazing panoramic view. As you climb the stairs you will be able to visit 8 floors which offer mini exhibits where you will learn how the lighthouse was built as well as the history of the lighthouse. If you are worried about the climb there is no need to be because there are several resting platforms for you on the way to the top of the light house. The lighthouse is still in use today even though most ships use much more sophisticated navigational methods such as GPS it is considered an extra line of defense to protect the ships from hitting the reefs off of the shoreline.
- St Catherine Fort- Surrounded by a dry moat St Catherine Fort is only accessible by Draw Bridge. This is where the crew of the Sea Venture first came to shore when their ship wrecked not far from the area in 1609. A small wooden fort was built in 1612 to help protect the island from Spanish attacks. It has since been renovated about five times and work was not completed on the fort until the late 19th century. Today the fort contains a museum and is known as one of the most impressive structures in Bermuda. You can also view an amazing collection of antique weapons that were used in Bermuda such as the five cannons that were used to protect the fort as well as a replica of the British crown jewels.

- Blue Hole Park & Walsingham Reserve- A beautiful reserve that is 12 acres is also known as Tom Moores jungle because it is where he wrote some of his poems under a calabash tree in 1844. The tree was destroyed by a hurricane in 1987 but the branches of the tree were replanted so that it could grow again. There are many caves and tunnels available for you to explore in the reserve and you can even enjoy the turtles and other sea life in the underwater caves. The reserve is located in Blue Hole Park which offers one of the most beautiful ponds in Bermuda. The pond has crystal clear blue water and is full of fish and marine life. There is also an observation deck that you can visit where you can watch birds stalk the marine life from shore.
- Dolphin Quest- I covered this just a little when talking about the Bermuda Aquarium, Museum & Zoo but would like to go in more depth about it because it is truly amazing. Originally opened in 1996 the Dolphin Quest is one of the most popular sites for tourists to visit in Bermuda. It is true that dolphins are wild animals and just like any other animal they can be dangerous if they are in a bad mood but the trainers at the Dolphin Quest are amazing and ensure that only the happy dolphins are allowed to interact with people each day. There are three different programs available offering between 20 to 45 minute swims with the dolphins and the prices range from 60 dollars to 225 dollars.

There are so many amazing sites for you to see in Bermuda but these are the best that are available. You can definitely fill up weeks of time visiting all of the amazing sites that are available in Bermuda.

Bermuda Tours & Excursions

When planning a trip to Bermuda you want to make sure that you choose the tour that is right for you and your family. In order to choose the right tour for you there are a few questions that you must answer first.

1. Do you want to spend your time walking and exploring Bermuda or would you rather have a guided bus, taxi or even boat tour? You may prefer to do a bit of both so that you enjoy as much of Bermuda as you can.

2. Would you like to explore the more off the beaten trail kind of places or would you like to visit places that are full of history? Is it the beaches that you want to visit or is it the sites? Maybe both.

It all depends on what you love to do and how you plan on spending your time in Bermuda.

Self-guided public transportation tours.

Bermuda is a small island so the chances of getting lost are very slim which means that you have the opportunity to use public transportation and explore the island a bit on your own. Using public transportation is the cheapest way for you to enjoy all that Bermuda has to offer but you must make sure you know exactly where you want to go and the fastest ways to get there in order to get the most out of your trip to Bermuda.

Boating and Sailing tours

Offering glass bottom views you will be able to enjoy the marine life and even visit shipwrecks when you take a boating tour in Bermuda. There are even dinner cruises that you can take where you will see all of the famous houses along the shore line. If you want something a bit more private you can also charter a private boat for you and your family.

Here are a few other types of tours available when visiting Bermuda.

Minibus tours- This is a great tour if you are traveling with a small group.

Taxi tours- Some of the taxi drivers in Bermuda are certified tour guides and each taxi can hold up to seven people so this is a great way to enjoy the sites with our family.

Walking and hiking tours- A great way to enjoy Bermuda's nature and enjoy all of the nooks and crannies of the island.

Horse carriage tours- There are three different stables that offer horse carriage tours and it is a great way to enjoy all that Bermuda has to offer.

Eco tours- Bermuda does offer several tours that are eco-friendly including bike tours, kayaking, and hiking tours.

Chapter 4
Bermuda Weather

The weather in Bermuda is something that you absolutely have to think about when you are planning a trip there. In the spring, fall, and winter the temperatures are usually mild and you can spend time enjoying the sites but in the summer the temperatures rise to around 90 degrees and the humidity is as high as 80 percent. Bermuda is usually snow and frost free because of the warm waters of the Gulf Stream that pass by Bermuda.

Bermuda is also a great place for those to visit that suffer with hay fever. Ragweed does not grow on the island and the pollen from other plant is blown out to sea very quickly. On the other hand those who suffer with allergies need to note that due to the damp conditions mold, mites, and mildew breed quickly.

The lowest air temperature ever recorded in Bermuda was 43 degrees and the high was 97. The area is also known for thunderstorms which are caused because of the wind coming off of the ocean. The month with the most rainfall in Bermuda is usually August where it rains 19 days out of the month and the month with the least rainfall is May when it only rains an average of 6 days out of the month.

The warmest months in Bermuda are July through October and the coldest month is February with an average temperature of 62 degrees. The average humidity year round is 77% but in the months of June, July, and August it is usually higher. During these months you may find that you need to change your clothes about three times a day because they will become saturated.

Hurricanes are part of life in Bermuda and many of the hotels carry a hurricane guarantee which states that in the event of canceled reservations due to a hurricane in the area all money will be refunded. You have to check with your hotel to see if they offer such a guarantee and if not you may want to go with a different hotel.

Studies have shown that a devastating hurricane hits the island every six to seven years on average and the hurricane season is May through October with most hurricanes occurring during the months of August, September, and October. When hurricanes to hit Bermuda the damage is often superficial compared to other areas that are hit by hurricanes.

Another thing that you need to consider when traveling to Bermuda is the fact that there are often electric outages because of the strong winds there. When this happens no water can be drawn unless it is done manually with buckets. It is reported that cable television can be out for over a month at time and the telephones can be out for weeks at a time.

Deciding when to travel to Bermuda

Deciding when you want to travel to Bermuda is very important depending on what type of experience you want to have. For example, the busy season is April through September and this is when all of the attractions and festivities are at their peak. This is also when the beaches are open. Although it is very crowded in Bermuda at this time, this is when you will be able to enjoy all of the entertainment available.

The slow season in Bermuda is between November and February and has its own advantages. The weather is much cooler during this time and the beaches as well as the hotels are much less crowded. You can even get special packages during this time that will save you a lot of money when in Bermuda. Some hotels even offer discounts up to 40% off during the off season months just so they are able to fill rooms. The fishing, swimming and snorkeling are just as enjoyable during these months as they are in the peak season and some would say even more so because of the lack of tourists at the time. The day time temperatures during the off season months are around 60 to 70 degrees and the evenings are a bit cooler so you need to remember to pack the right clothing if you visit during this time of the year.

It does not matter if you visit during the busy tourist season or if you visit during the off months, you are sure to have a great time in Bermuda and will have no problem filling your days with exciting adventures.

Chapter 5
Why Go To Bermuda?

You may be wondering why you should travel to Bermuda when there are so many other destinations in the world that you can travel to. One of the main reasons that people travel to Bermuda, especially those from the United States is that it is so close to home but it feels like it is a million miles away.

You are able to enjoy all of the different customs in Bermuda without having to worry about being too far from home in the event of an emergency. Which helps many who are just beginning to travel to relax and be able to enjoy their experience.

If you are thinking about going to Bermuda for your honeymoon you could not choose a better place. Bermuda offers a great back drop for those who are just beginning their lives together and there is no place quite as romantic as the island.

Another reason why you should consider visiting Bermuda is because of the amazing history that is has. As we discussed in chapter one Bermuda has had its struggles and it is a great way to get in touch with history.

Bermuda also offers so many options when it comes to taking vacation there. There is something for everyone when it comes to Bermuda from the beautiful beaches to the fantastic night life you will find so many things that you enjoy while you are there.

Most people who visit Bermuda find themselves returning again and again because there is not only so much to explore but there are such wonderful customs in the area. When you visit Bermuda you get to take part in all of the festivities and learn about how those on the island live their day to day life.

There is a wonderful man named John who spends each of his mornings walking around Bermuda saying hello to all the locals and new visitors. You definitely won't find that kind of hospitality at any other vacation destination!

Mark Twain talking about Bermuda said, "You can go to heaven if you want but I want to stay here."

Chapter 6
Tips and Warnings When Traveling to Bermuda.

In this chapter I want to discuss some tips and warnings for you when you are traveling to Bermuda. First I want to talk about the warnings, these are all the things that you should be aware of when you are traveling to Bermuda in order to keep yourself and your family out of danger and safe.

Warning
The first thing I want to talk about is the traffic hazards in Bermuda, it is very important to know these hazards so that you do not put your life at risk.

- For the most part when you travel through Bermuda you will find that the roads are very old and have not been redone. You must be very careful on these roads because they were not made for large vehicles.

- If you can drive in Bermuda you can drive anywhere. Driving in Bermuda is not for the faint of heart. It is very crowded and there is a lot of traffic. People are also quite aggressive when driving in Bermuda so if you choose to drive yourself be very cautious but it is better to hire a taxi to drive you.

- Renting a Motorbike is very dangerous. Although it is an option when you travel to Bermuda, renting a Motorbike can be very dangerous because there is so much traffic on the roads in Bermuda and because most that visit are not used to driving on the left side of the road there are over 500 motor bike accidents per year.

- If you do plan on driving you should be warned that gas prices are extremely high in Bermuda. Those from Europe will not be as surprised as those from the US because the price is literally double that of gas in the US.

- Speed limits throughout the entire island are between 15 and 20 miles per hour and it is very important that you obey and pay attention to them. There are so many people traveling on foot and on bike in Bermuda you do not want to be the cause for any accidents.

- Sidewalks are virtually nonexistent in Bermuda except for in town. This is not much of a problem during the day because they are easily visible to those who are driving but if you are walking around at night you need to make sure that you can be seen because the roads are narrow and if a driver does not know you are there until the last second he or she has no place to go.

- Another reason you should be careful at night is because many in Bermuda are lax about drinking and driving and many tourist are hurt or killed each year in accidents involving alcohol. Even though you may think it is the norm to drink and drive in Bermuda don't do it, there are taxis available at each and every bar so make sure you take one back to your hotel.

Warnings about the weather

As silly as it may seem there are even some warnings that you should remember about the weather. Here are a few.

- Don't travel around the island when it is storming. It is not safe and the winds alone can be damaging. Make sure you check the weather before you go out and if it is going to storm be sure to call a taxi service.
- Make sure you pay attention to the weather reports especially during hurricane season. Few hurricanes actually hit Bermuda because of its size but it is important to not only pay attention to the current weather forecast but also the long-term forecast.

Shopping In Bermuda

There is not much that can be said about the shopping in Bermuda because there really are not that many places for tourists to shop. The places that are available for shoppers are extremely expensive so my tip to you when it comes to shopping in Bermuda is to wait until you get back home.

The Beaches of Bermuda

Bermuda is a great place to swim, dive and snorkel as well as enjoy the beaches but there are a few warnings you should be aware of before attempting any of these.

- Of course you should always protect yourself from the sun especially when you are on the Bermuda beaches. Make sure you and your children apply lots of sunscreen you wouldn't want to be mistaken for a lobster and ruin your entire visit.
- On the beaches and in the water there is one very toxic jelly fish. This jelly fish is called the Man of Water and is blue in color. It can sting you even after it has died and washed up on the beach and the venom is 75% the toxicity of the cobra. The most common time to see these jelly fish is in the early spring or in the summer and especially after there has been a storm. It is also important to know that their tentacles can reach up to 150 feet in length so even if you don't see the fish the tentacles could be nearby.

- Even though the beaches can be lots of fun you must also remain aware that there can be some very dangerous riptides at times. If you are not used to being on the beach this is something that could put you in a lot of danger. There are lifeguards on duty if you do get in a dangerous situation but it is always best to use common sense before going out into the ocean. So if it looks dangerous to you, stay away.

Tips for traveling in Bermuda

One of the things that you have to remember when you are traveling in Bermuda is that the locals are very friendly. Tourism is how the island earns most of its money and the locals respect that and understand that without tourism they could not continue with their way of life. With all of that said you need to remember to be polite back. If you are found being impolite in Bermuda many off the locals will shake their finger at you or correct you. You can even get looked over purposely when wanting some type of service such as ordering your dinner if the locals feel that you are being rude to them.

The second thing you should know about Bermuda is that it is okay to drink the water. Many times tourists are afraid to drink the water when they are traveling but Bermuda's water is perfectly safe for you to enjoy.

Make sure you get a good map of Bermuda when you travel there. It may be a small island but the fact is that you want to know exactly where everything is and the shortest routes to get where you want to go. You don't want to end up wasting half of your vacation or honeymoon because you got lost or could not find the place you were looking for. And if all else fails don't be afraid to ask for directions, remember the locals are very friendly.

You should also remember that even though Bermuda is a very safe place for you to travel crime can happen anywhere. For that reason make sure you carry your purse and camera in a backpack when you are traveling through Bermuda. Make sure that you only take the amount of money that you will need with you and leave everything else that you do not need back in your safe in your hotel room. There is a very low crime rate in Bermuda but you should remember that does not mean that it never happens. Keep your eyes open and know your surroundings. You should watch for anyone who looks suspicious and make sure you are not off wondering on your own.

It is very safe for women to travel alone when they are in Bermuda due to the low crime rate. Even though it is safe for women to be alone you want to make sure you let someone know where you are going at all times and when you plan on returning. Even if you are just sending an email to a friend back home they will be able to contact the authorities if something were to happen to you .

Make sure you take any medical care items that you need with you. It is possible to find what you will need on the island but it is very expensive to purchase medical items there and you will want to spend your money on other things while there.

You should not take any firearms or knifes with you when traveling to Bermuda because it is currently against the law to have them in your possession in Bermuda.

English is the main language that is spoken in Bermuda and although there are other languages spoken by the locals you will have no trouble communicating with most of them.

Make sure you make plans for proper accommodations while you will be in Bermuda. There are hotels, bed and breakfasts, and even cottages that you can rent. One thing you should note is that even though you may see people camping while you are in Bermuda tourist are not allowed to do so. Only the local population can camp in Bermuda.

If you like seafood you will love the food in Bermuda. The food is caught by local fishermen and sold to the restaurants and markets the same day. You will also be able to find a lot of English restaurants all over the island.

You cannot buy a one way ticket to Bermuda. If you want to gain entry to Bermuda you must purchase a round trip ticket. Your passport must also be up to date as well as show that you are a citizen and retain the right to reenter your country.

You should know that you can use the US dollar in Bermuda and there are plenty of ATM's located all over the island so you do not have to worry about carrying a lot of cash with you as you are out exploring. You will want to take some cash with you though because it is a great way to obtain tons of bargains from the locals.

Before traveling to Bermuda make sure you check out the travel deal websites. You can find a lot of great deals on trips to Bermuda as well as hotels by simply searching these sites. It only takes a few minutes and could save you hundreds of dollars. And we all know it would not matter how much money you had you don't want to waste any of it.

Those are all of the tips and warnings while visiting Bermuda that I have for you. The most important tip I can give you when it comes to visiting Bermuda is to make sure you plan your trip out in advance, you want to have some type of plan or you will find yourself wonder all over the island for hours at a time not really finding anything enjoyable to do. Set a schedule, and know where your destinations are as well as the fastest route to get to each one of them. Make sure not one minute is wasted while you are in Bermuda and make sure you take the time to visit the beautiful beaches and spend some time relaxing on them.

Conclusion

Thank you again for downloading this book!

Finally, if you enjoyed this book, please take the time to share your thoughts and post a review on Amazon. It'd be greatly appreciated!

Thank you and good luck!

Check Out My Other Books

Below you'll find some of my other popular books that are popular on Amazon and Kindle as well. Simply click on the links below to check them out. Alternatively, you can visit my author page on Amazon to see other work done by me.

If the links do not work, for whatever reason, you can simply search for these titles on the Amazon website to find them.